Jean Keyes

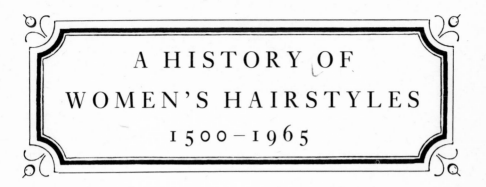

A HISTORY OF
WOMEN'S HAIRSTYLES
1500–1965

METHUEN & CO LTD
11 NEW FETTER LANE · LONDON EC4

First published 1967 by Methuen & Co. Ltd,
11 New Fetter Lane, London EC4
© 1967 Jean Keyes
Reprinted 1968
Phototypeset in Great Britain
by BAS Printers Limited, Over Wallop, Hampshire
and printed in Great Britain
by Cox and Wyman Limited, Fakenham

WITHDRAWN

A HISTORY OF
WOMEN'S HAIRSTYLES
1500–1965

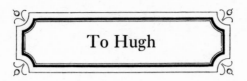

To Hugh

Contents

Foreword   *page* ix

Hairstyles   1

Accessories and Jewellery   69

List of books, periodicals and museums
   used for reference   81

Suggestions for further sources of information   83

Index   85

Foreword

In this age of rapidly changing styles, it is sometimes difficult to imagine life without magazines, television or films, which convey fashion to us. However, since these inventions have all developed within the last fifty or sixty years, you must cast your mind back beyond that period to try to imagine the life of ladies in earlier years.

The mass of my information has been obtained from miniatures and portraits and it has not been until later years that I have been able to use fashion plates. Miniatures and painted portraits are often the only record that we have today of the changes of styling that have taken place through the centuries.

To write this book, which originally started as teaching notes, I have therefore had to rely for the most part on information about the wealthier people of previous centuries. The aristocracy and members of society were the people most able to afford, and most likely to commission, a portrait or miniature. Occasionally miniatures of tradespeople are seen, but these are not common and are usually of women who would follow fashion as best they could. Information on the middle and lower classes is therefore hard to obtain until this century.

When I have found illustrations of middle class hairstyles, I have included them on the appropriate pages of drawings. Sometimes, therefore, one can see a style which seems 'old-fashioned' in comparison with others on that page. This is because by the time the latest style had reached either middle class people or landed gentry in the remoter parts of the country, the court circle was indulging in another whim—adding a puff or curl, shaving the head and wearing a wig, introducing 'small' heads, 'large' heads, or simply tying up the hair with a ribbon for a casual effect and thus creating a new style which would then be copied by hundreds of eager women.

On looking through the following pages, one can see a definite trend. A style becomes more and more extravagant or grotesque, until it seems that every change and alteration possible has been made and everyone is becoming a little bored with the effect. Then often within a few months a change is made—frequently a completely new silhouette is tried and away they all go again, with milliners, jewellers and hairdressers all making new creations to suit the trend.

Of course, this is the nature of women everywhere, and what used to take several years to evolve now takes perhaps a season.

One of the amusing things to notice whilst looking back in time is the latent desire for uniformity which seems to have been always present within us. You choose a style which you may feel to be different, unusual, even unique, but it takes only a casual glance at an old group photograph to see how closely you in fact followed the trend of the time.

We note the court circle copying Queen Elizabeth I in her hair colour and in her desire for many wigs, but were these whims followed as a desire to compliment or because of the natural fear of being 'out of step'?

In later years, the young Duchesse de Fontanges, a favourite of the French king Louis XIV, tied up her wind-swept hair with a ribbon whilst out riding and was complimented, unconsciously starting a new fashion. Did the ladies who were present at that time hope that they too would be complimented and perhaps win favour with King Louis XIV, or did they all think it was such a good idea at the same time?

We can also see in modern times how the teenagers of today copy the style of a particular film star or pop singer, not necessarily because they genuinely feel that the style suits them, but possibly because a little reflected glory may be passed on to them.

Thus fashion evolves, started by a whim, a casual act, a political event or a youth strumming a guitar, and usually ended by inconvenience, difficulty or boredom.

Fashion can be dull, grotesque, flattering or laughable, but to any woman who is concerned with her appearance, it is always interesting.

Hairstyles

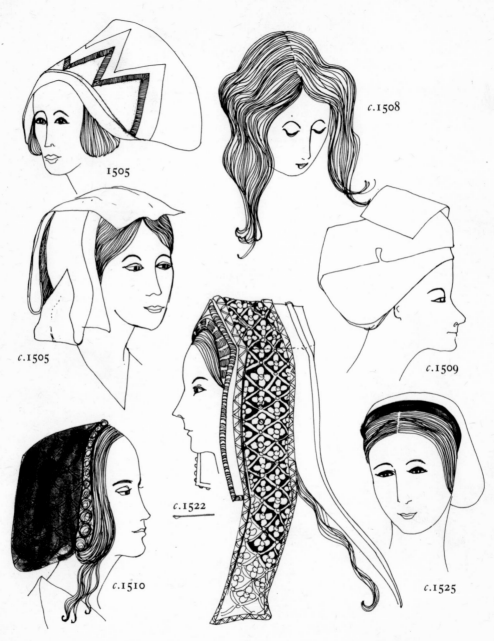

1505

c.1508

c.1505

c.1509

c.1510

c.1522

c.1525

2

Hair had been concealed under head-dresses for many years, and at the beginning of the sixteenth century this fashion was still in force. However, in most of these styles a small portion of hair was visible, and it can be seen that the hair was usually parted in the middle and draped down the side of the face and round the ears to form a smooth effect. The way that the style contrasted with the often quite elaborate head-dresses made it a fitting one.

Head-dresses differed widely in shape and in the way in which they were made; some were a construction of folded white linen or lawn (these are still seen today in various forms worn by nuns), and some were of a more complicated nature, often covered with rich embroidery and encrusted with jewels.

The custom for young unmarried girls and brides to wear their hair loose and flowing persisted at the beginning of this century. Alternatively, long hair was sometimes braided, and often a bride would wear a *coif* of silk or a circlet of flowers, which might have been either real or of enamelled silver.

SOURCES OF INFORMATION

Wood Carvings, Victoria and Albert Museum
Francis Kelly and Randolph Schwabe, *Historic Costume* (Batsford)
Mary Houston, *Mediaeval Costume in England and France* (Adam and Charles Black)

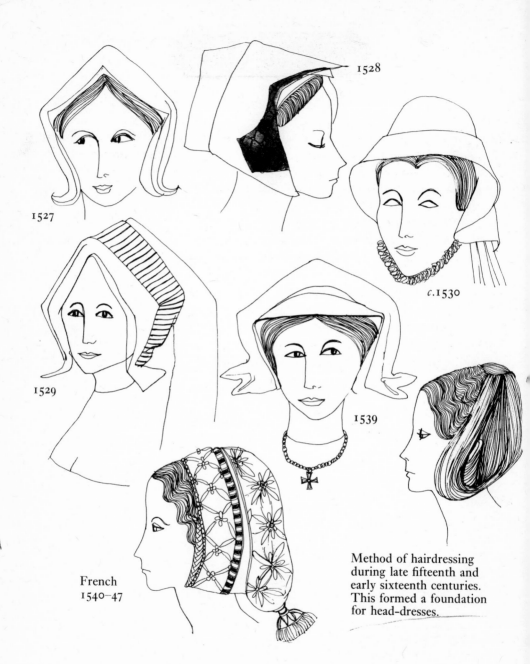

1527

1528

c.1530

1529

1539

French
1540–47

Method of hairdressing
during late fifteenth and
early sixteenth centuries.
This formed a foundation
for head-dresses.

4

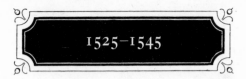

During this period hairstyles seem to have remained unchanged. Hair was used merely to form a foundation for the head-dress. Head-dresses differed in shape from those of the previous twenty years and were mainly caps of white linen. A middle parting is seen in most cases, presumably to complete the symmetrical effect of the head-dress.

An illustration shows how the hair was dressed to support the head-dress. From a central parting, the hair was drawn back and fastened at the back of the head, then draped down to the nape of the neck, round in front of the ears and back to the top of the head again. There it was fastened in a small knot. An alternative style for hair that was not quite so long would have been to drape the hair, from a middle parting, under the ears and fasten it at the back of the head. However, for both styles long hair was necessary, and therefore we can presume that hair was not often cut after girlhood.

SOURCES OF INFORMATION

Mary Houston, *Mediaeval Costume in England and France* (Adam and Charles Black)
Francis Kelly and Randolph Schwabe, *Historic Costume* (Batsford)

c.1548

1551

mid 1500s

1577

1565

1560

6

By 1550 the fashion of *frizzing* the hair had arrived from France. This was probably done in a similar way to modern 'back-combing', the hair then being brushed over pads and wire frames to hold out the style on the temples. The French version, the *Attifet Coiffure*, was copied in England; in the Venetian version the hair was built up into two horns.

Hair was kept in place with a sticky paste. Gum or mucelage was expensive and therefore used only by the upper classes, other people having to make do with paste made from the dust of rotten oak or from flour.

False hair was added when necessary: a set of false ringlets or curls was called a *wig*, a full head of hair known as a *periwig* or *peruke*.

The illustrations show the beginning of the transition from wearing head-dresses of interesting shapes to making the hair itself an interesting shape. By 1560 head-dresses were growing smaller and showing more hair than ever.

Powdering the hair became popular during this period, pale violet, white and pale yellow being fashionable shades.

Cosmetics: 'face painting', as it was then called, was first introduced in the French court, and was done in the same way as painting pictures. The fashion for evening was for bright red cheeks on a coating of white paint. During the day a delicate pallor was fashionable, probably from necessity since the paints had a harmful effect on the skin, counteracted by cooling lotions.

Masks became popular during the 1540s, originally being small pieces of gauze lining hung below the eyes. The Venetian or *loup* (wolf) mask, so called because it frightened children, was of black velvet lined with white satin.

SOURCES OF INFORMATION

Mary Houston, *Mediaeval Costume in England and France* (Adam and Charles Black)
Francis Kelly and Randolph Schwabe, *Historic Costume* (Batsford)

c.1575

1575—80

1571

1565

1571

1570—80

1571

1570—80

8

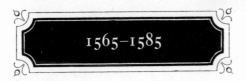

By 1565 head-dresses had shrunk to a mere bonnet size and into a shape that was a compliment to the hair shape. Here the *ruff* worn around the neck is seen for the first time, and was to achieve great popularity. These ruffs were made in various shapes and sizes; they rose high at the back of the neck. Therefore hair had to be kept out of the way and was consequently short at the nape of the neck but high in the front. It was built out on pads in the same manner as in the previous twenty years and also fixed with gum or other sticky substances.

Hair and wigs were powdered; this may have been done to counteract the stickiness of the pastes.

Face painting continued and was very popular, although the corrosive effects of the heavy painting often showed.

Masks were still worn over the face to protect the make-up whilst outside. A full-face mask with eye holes, made of black or green silk, was often worn. This was kept in place by a button, fastened on the inside of the mask and held between the teeth.

SOURCES OF INFORMATION

Strömbom, *Index över Svenska Porträtt 1500–1850* (Catalogues of Stockholm National Museum)
Francis Kelly and Randolph Schwabe, *Historic Fashion* (Batsford)
Mary Houston, *Mediaeval Costume in England and France* (Adam and Charles Black)
National Portrait Gallery

c.1600

1600

1595–1600

1589

1600

c.1600

c.1600

Periwigs had become popular by this time. Hair was by now so complicated to dress and so uncomfortable to wear that most ladies had their heads shaved and wore a complete periwig. Queen Elizabeth had as many as eighty dyed periwigs, her favourite colours being auburn or saffron yellow, although she was naturally blonde. This of course set the fashion in court, and most of the court ladies had their periwigs dyed similar shades.

Periwigs were mostly made up of either tiny curls or hair frizzed into tiny waves. They were built up into a variety of shapes, usually symmetrical and often with a pronounced peak in the centre of the forehead. On this page, however, there are two illustrations showing the hair still in straighter styles. These would be achieved, as in previous years, by a 'back-combing' process and would probably also be periwigs.

The periwigs were decorated with pearls, jewels and feathers, or sometimes lace edgings and trims.

Hair by now was extremely precious and would often be stolen from children and young girls.

SOURCES OF INFORMATION

Strömbom, *Index över Svenska Porträtt 1500–1850* (Catalogues of Stockholm National Museum)
Miniatures, Victoria and Albert Museum

1605

1615

1605

c.1615

c.1620

c.1612

1623

1610

12

The fashion for small curls continued for a time but the general height of hairstyles lessened, although the hair seldom hung below the ear lobes. The natural hair was built over pads (the fashion for periwigs was dwindling as styles became more manageable). A variety of styles became popular by 1605, as some ladies changed to the more natural look. The hair was coiled into a *bun* high at the back of the head and then almost covered by a small coif (head-dress), from which only a curled *fringe* and a few *ringlets* showed. Another version was to drape the hair away from a middle parting, and coil it into a bun at the back of the head, covered by a veil.

By 1610 a style involving an arched wire support, over which the hair was brushed to form a knife edge, was popular. This was often combined with a row of small curls as a fringe.

By 1623 a definite change to the more natural look could be seen and, although the actual outline of the style had not changed, the crimped look of 1615 and before had obviously lost its appeal.

SOURCES OF INFORMATION

Miniatures, Victoria and Albert Museum
Prints, Victoria and Albert Museum

13

1628

c.1630

1630–40

1640

c.1636

c.1640

c.1638

c.1642

1642

14

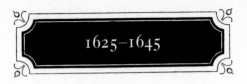

A complete change can now be seen. The natural hair is again used completely and a variety of natural styles achieved.

From 1625 the back hair was coiled into a bun and the side hair left to fall from two side partings into ringlets, curls or a frizz. A small curled fringe was often popular and the top hair was kept close to the head.

By 1638 more complicated styles were fashionable, with many ringlets at the side. Styles now start to become assymetrical, with either a different arrangement of ringlets on each side, or rolls of curls on one side and ringlets on the other. Sometimes, as in the example for *c*.1640, these puffs, rolls and ringlets would be built out over a pad, the whole head of hair being quite short with the exception of one long ringlet to trail over one shoulder.

Hair decorations were mostly confined to ribbons twisted around the buns or amongst the ringlets.

Face patches were popular by 1640, and were made of velvet or silk and stuck onto the face.

SOURCES OF INFORMATION

Strömbom, *Index över Svenska Porträtt 1500–1850* (Catalogues of Stockholm National Museum)
Miniatures, Victoria and Albert Museum
National Portrait Gallery

c.1648

1656

c.1660

c.1650

c.1660

c.1660

1655

c.1660

1661

c.1660

16

Styles followed much the same trend for the next ten years. Curled fringes were still seen until about 1660, but by then most ladies had restricted the fringe to a single, small curling ringlet falling over the forehead. The top of the head was kept flat and the back hair formed into ringlets on either side of the face to shoulder level.

Two examples can be seen of the back of the head. Both of these appear to have the hair pulled back to form a coiled bun with the long ends of hair circling the bun and fastened with ribbons. The circle of hair could have been a false piece, added if the natural hair were not long enough.

A variety of methods of dressing the back hair can be seen c.1660, where it is coiled into buns of many shapes, often decorated with strings of pearls. Sometimes the back hair was lifted to the centre of the head and then curled over into ringlets.

Assymetrical styles were popular, often with the hair cut to different lengths in order to achieve them.

SOURCES OF INFORMATION

Francis Kelly and Randolph Schwabe, *Historic Costume* (Batsford)
National Portrait Gallery
Miniatures, Victoria and Albert Museum

1665-75

c.1670

1669

c.1670

c.1680

1665

1675

c.1672

18

An example of *'wired-out' curls* can be seen here for 1669. The curls were arranged on wires to stand away from the head and sometimes strings of pearls would be entwined in them. The back hair would be arranged in a bun and there would be one or two ringlets of back hair coming forward over the shoulders.

Another example of 'wired-out' curls can be seen *c.*1670, where bunches of ringlets are wired out to each side over the ears.

A style which became popular in the 1670s was that of close curls all over the front and sides of the head, with the back hair made into ringlets to hang forward over the shoulders.

Apart from these new styles, the other fashions continued as they had in previous years. Although many of these styles look a little haphazard in their arrangement, the effect was one of calculated untidyness. In fact, many of the curls and ringlets, whether real or false, had their own names:

Confidants were the small curls near the ears.

Crève-Coeurs (heart-breakers) were small curls near the nape of the neck.

Cruches were small curls forming a fringe on the forehead.

Favourites were ringlets dangling from the side of the face.

A *Passagère* was a curl at the temple.

SOURCES OF INFORMATION

Strömbom, *Index över Svenska Porträtt 1500–1850* (Catalogues of Stockholm National Museum)
Francis Kelly and Randolph Schwabe, *Historic Costume* (Batsford)
Miniatures, Victoria and Albert Museum

c.1700

c.1680

1689–94

Lady with
mask 1689

c.1700

1690–1700

1685

1688

As well as the old styles which continued, various new styles could be recognized during this period. One, particularly popular from 1690 onwards, was that of curls wired above the forehead. Sometimes these were arranged in two peaks, the back hair being brought forward in two long ringlets.

The back hair from about 1685 was not often made into a bun but more generally into ringlets.

The new fashion from about 1690 onwards was that of the 'Tower' (*Tour*). This was a short-lived fashion, as it went out of favour by 1710, and it was very often worn with a high lace head-dress called a *fontange*. Court hair was curled and built up over 'rolls', and sometimes worn with favourites. The back hair was again coiled into a bun, leaving a few strands of hair to fall forward over the shoulders.

An illustration on this page shows a cape hood which has been made very high in order to cover the Tower and *fontange* without crushing them.

Powdering the hair was still popular.

SOURCES OF INFORMATION

Strömbom, *Index över Svenska Porträtt 1500–1850* (Catalogues of Stockholm National Museum)
Francis Kelly and Randolph Schwabe, *Historic Costume* (Batsford)
National Portrait Gallery
Miniatures, Victoria and Albert Museum

c.1710

1710

c.1705

1710

1703

1700

c.1710

22

During this period there was not much change in styles. Powdered hair was still fashionable and, for the first few years, the hair was piled high in sweeping curves with the back hair falling into a long ringlet.

A development of the *fontange* can be seen here, where it has become a kind of cap.

The Hanover cut was popular on the Continent but never appealed in England. This was a variation of the Tower: the hair was dressed in a semi-circle over the forehead, and decorated with gauze and ribbon. This was then plastered with pomatum and powder.

From 1720 onwards working women wore a simple style which is illustrated here. The front hair was loosely waved about the face and the back hair made into a bun high on the back of the head.

SOURCES OF INFORMATION

Francis Kelly and Randolph Schwabe, *Historic Costume* (Batsford)
Miniatures, Victoria and Albert Museum
National Portrait Gallery

1740

1729

1730

1731

1730

1731

1739

1736

c.1735

1744

1745

24

Hair was generally much shorter at this period and fell into the following categories. The front hair was swept up and back to form a roll from ear to ear over the forehead; the back hair would either be made into a roll from ear to ear around the nape of the neck, or into a high, flat bun. These styles were decorated with either ribbons or flowers.

Tête-de-Mouton (sheep's-head) was the name given to a style made up of short false curls worn on the back of the head and falling towards the forehead and temples. An example is seen on this page for 1736.

Periwigs were worn for horse-riding and also at court and for other social occasions.

Mob-caps were popular, particularly with the elderly. As they covered the hair completely, they were an ideal compromise for anyone not wishing to follow fashion.

SOURCES OF INFORMATION

Strömbom, *Index över Svenska Porträtt 1500–1850* (Catalogues of Stockholm National Museum)
Miniatures, Victoria and Albert Museum
National Portrait Gallery
Francis Kelly and Randolph Schwabe, *Historic Costume* (Batsford)

1750

1755

1745

1740

1759

1760

1760

1761

1756

1760

26

Hairstyles were low and insignificant during the first ten years of this period.

The front hair was generally combed straight back from the forehead and temples, but the back of the style could be dressed in several ways. These were as follows:

a) Turned up and twisted into a flat bun.

b) Made into a plait, either to twist round the head or to hang down the back. Other varieties were the *Tête-de-Mouton* style (although this became unfashionable by the 1750s) or one with the back hair cut short.

With the exception of some court styles, the neck was exposed. The court styles followed the fashions of previous years by dressing the hair high in the front, the back hair being allowed to fall forward into ringlets.

Hairstyles were often decorated with pearls or flowers, and often head-dresses in the shape of mob-caps or a small bonnet tying under the chin were worn.

The close, feminine styles of this period seem to be a direct opposite to the men's styles, which had reached the extreme in large periwigs.

SOURCES OF INFORMATION

Strömbom, *Index över Svenska Porträtt 1500–1850* (Catalogues of Stockholm National Museum)
Miniatures, Victoria and Albert Museum
National Portrait Gallery

1781

1772

Cartoon
1777 ✓

1779

French
1779

c.1773

1770

1790–1800

28

By 1765, however, fashions were more extravagant and the hair raised from the forehead on pads of wool or horse hair. False hair might be added, in small curls one above the other on the temples. By 1768 the hair was puffed out over a roll and knotted on top of the head. The *'toupee'* gradually increased in height until it often exceeded the length of the ⸱⸱⸱ ⸱he arrangements being either egg-shaped or half-moon-shaped, with large ⸱⸱⸱ ⸱⸱ntally on the temples at either side. The back of the ⸱⸱⸱ long loop of hair hanging from the top and looped ⸱⸱⸱

During this period the follow ⸱⸱⸱ used: *cushions—* large pads filled with horse hair or wool; rolls ⸱⸱⸱ of varying sizes; wire supports. These were uncomfortable to wear and caused headaches. The false hair was dressed over them and plastered with paste or *pomatum*. The styles soon became objectionable as it was impossible to comb them, they were too complicated to take down every night, and washing hair was still a twice-yearly event. This soon became unbearable, and many ladies had their heads shaved and wore periwigs in the same styles. Shown opposite is an extreme version from a cartoon. In 1775 Maria Theresa wrote to her daughter, Marie Antoinette:

'. . . they say that your coiffure rises thirty-six inches . . . and is decorated with a mass of feathers and ribbons, which make it even higher. . . . I was always of the opinion that one should follow the fashions with restraint but never exaggerate them.'

SOURCES OF INFORMATION

G. Aretz, *The Elegant Woman* (George Harrap)
Miniatures, Victoria and Albert Museum

1785

1785

1785

1787

1790

1787

c.1790

1795

1793

1790

Here slight modifications may be seen, with styles generally lower at the top. The hair tends to be swept up onto the top of the head and tied into a small bun, the loose ends being allowed to fall into ringlets at the back.

Two examples for 1787 show the extremes affected by actresses of the period; in these styles, the curls would be stiffened either with wire or with paste in order to make them stand out. Large gauzy mob-caps were popular, perched on these styles and decorated with large bows of ribbon.

An example for 1790 shows the front hair cut short and curled close to the head, while the back hair is arranged in curls and ringlets. Sometimes this style would be arranged with a *chignon flotant*, one or more loops of hair hanging down the back, similar to styles of previous years.

An example for 1793 shows ringlets all over the head and falling at the back of the neck; this style is worn with a bandeau of white organza.

Wigs were only occasionally worn.

SOURCES OF INFORMATION

National Portrait Gallery
Miniatures, Victoria and Albert Museum

1800

1795

1795

1803

Child *c.*1800

*c.*1800

1800

1800

1804

1802

1800

1801

32

For the first five years of this period fashions continued in the same styles as previously. There was a growing popularity in styles with the top hair cut short but leaving the fringe longer than the top hair. The fringe was either arranged in regular curls across the forehead or allowed to hang in an almost haphazard fashion. The back hair would either be caught up into a bunch on the top of the head or arranged in coils down the back of the head.

In an example dated 1795 on this page, false curls attached to a *bandeau* have been added from ear to ear across the forehead; these were arranged in regular curls to match the curls of natural hair forming the fringe.

By 1800 the trend was definitely towards shorter hair. The untidy fringes remained, but the side and back hair was either cut to just below ear level or arranged in a close chignon so that it just covered the ears.

The 'dishevelled' look was extremely popular during this period and was influenced by France, where new fashions were started after the monarchy was overthrown.

SOURCES OF INFORMATION

Miniatures, Victoria and Albert Museum
Strömbom, *Index över Svenska Porträtt 1500–1850* (Catalogues of Stockholm National Museum)
National Portrait Gallery

1810

1811

1810

1805

1810–17

1810

1810

1812

1805

1810

1812

The 'dishevelled look' continued and hair by this time was mainly short. Sometimes the short hair was arranged in small curls all over the head, and sometimes allowed to remain almost straight and cut in different lengths to form a really ragged look.

By 1810, however, the 'dishevelled look' had passed and hair was being worn much longer, sometimes in small ringlets hanging down the neck but mostly in a variety of chignons. By now the word '*chignon*' was used for an arrangement of hair pinned high on the back or side of the head.

On this page, several variations of the chignon can be seen, either arranged in rolls, or with plaits or curls as decoration.

The fashion for fringes continued but in the main these were more regulated than those of previous years. Decorative bandeaux were sometimes worn and hats were taking the *bonnet* shape.

SOURCES OF INFORMATION

Strömbom, *Index över Svenska Porträtt 1500–1850* (Catalogues of Stockholm National Museum)
Miniatures, Victoria and Albert Museum
Fashion Plates, Victoria and Albert Museum

1815

1815

1816

1820

1815-20

Spanish
fancy
dress
1819

1820

1815-22

36

Hair was now worn longer and with a profusion of hair ornaments, from full-blown roses to ostrich feathers and jewelled stars. In 1815 the hair was crimped and curled in ringlets about the face with the back hair swept up into a chignon. Over this would be worn decorative *hats* and bandeaux, so that in many cases most of the hair was hidden.

An alternative to these styles was an arrangement of ringlets and sausage curls all over the head, topped by full-blown roses—1816.

By 1820 hair was longer and usually piled high at the back into a variety of unusually shaped chignons. The front hair was either short and set in tiny curls, or longer and set into bunches of ringlets over each temple. Coiled *plaits* (probably of false hair) were a popular way of fastening a chignon on top of the head. These would be wrapped around the hair to form a large bun.

An example dated 1820 shows an evening style where the back hair has been drawn onto the top of the head and arranged in ringlets, with the front and side hair arranged in small curls. The whole style was fastened with a bandeau, to which was attached an arrangement of ostrich plumes standing high above the head.

SOURCES OF INFORMATION

Stephané, *L'Art de la Coiffure Féminine* (*Édition de 'La Coiffure de Paris'*)
Miniatures, Victoria and Albert Museum
Fashion Plates, Victoria and Albert Museum

c. 1828

1825

1827

1828

1830

1833

1825

1835

38

1825–1835

The chignon was still popular and the arrangement of false hair pieces (as in the illustration c.1828) common. For evening wear the decorations remained on the hair, but for day wear hats were the focal point and were extremely large and over-decorated.

The hair underneath the hats would be arranged in a simple chignon, swept round from a central parting. The fashion for large hats did not last long and by 1827 more interesting day styles can be seen.

Ringlets and roll curls were still frequently worn and were arranged on either side of the face in an assymetric style. By 1830 the bunches on either side of the face had increased in breadth and shortened in length.

For evening wear, the styles were extravagant throughout this period. The basic style remained similar, however, and was made up of bunches of curls or ringlets on each temple and a high looped chignon at the back of the head. These styles would then be decorated with leaves, flowers, lace veils or ribbon bows.

SOURCES OF INFORMATION

Miniatures, Victoria and Albert Museum
Fashion Plates, Victoria and Albert Museum

1835

1836

1839

1840

1836

1841

1842 Cartoon

1842

1839

1840

40

1835–1845

Braids were popular again in 1835 as decoration. Two examples may be seen on this page, one style showing braids made into a looped-up bow on top of the head, the other with braids forming a circlet on top of the head and ringlets falling over the ears from the temples.

Bunches of curls or ringlets from the temples were popular from 1836 onwards, the top hair being pulled back to form a chignon on the back of the head. The bunches of curls fell from two side partings.

Another variation of this style is seen in the cartoon of 1842, where the artist has made a comparison between the style and the long ears of a spaniel. By this time middle partings were fashionable and were to stay so for twenty years. Another style for 1842 was one with the hair swept under the ears and forming ringlets behind the ears. The ringlets in this illustration were held in place by roses. An example dated 1840 is similar but with strings of pearls coiled into the hair.

The most noticeable point about the styles from 1840 onwards was that the top hair was sleek and flat, the fullness being over the ears.

SOURCES OF INFORMATION

Fashion Plates
Costume Gallery, Victoria and Albert Museum
Punch History of Manners and Modes
Miniatures, Victoria and Albert Museum

1845

1850

1845

1845

1852

1852

1845

1845

1845

1853

1855

1854

42

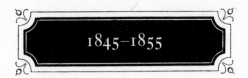

Variations of the previous ten years' fashions can be seen here. The top hair remained sleek, the variations coming mainly in the arrangement of the side ringlets. These were achieved in the following ways: by having ringlets on one side only, by plaiting the hair instead of making ringlets and by tucking the hair back with no ringlets at all.

These, however, were only variations and in 1855 side ringlets were still in evidence. Examples on this page show more complicated versions of the chignon as either a large coiled bun, a complex knot or two loops similar to those of the previous century.

Bonnets were made to sit on top of these styles, the *poke bonnet* still being popular as the back was so accommodating for large chignons. False hair pieces were often used to form extra layers of ringlets or curls where necessary. These would be obtained in the form of a cluster and attached to the natural hair with a comb or hairpin.

SOURCES OF INFORMATION

Fashion Plates, Victoria and Albert Museum

1855

1860

1855

1857

1860

1860

1863

1865

44

1855–1865

Styles changed again during this period, although the top hair was kept sleek and middle partings were still popular.

It was the back of the head, therefore, which showed the changes. One style was made up of vertical sausage-shaped curls at the back of the head; another was that of sweeping the hair round into a large puff dressing, with or without a long ringlet hanging down the back. There are two examples of this style, one dated 1860 with additional ringlets, the other dated 1855 with braided trimming over the top of the head.

Yet another variation was that of sweeping the hair to the back of the head with a braided coil around the head. Sometimes a false cluster of curls was attached at the nape of the neck for added interest.

An example dated 1863 shows the back view of a very simple style, where the hair has been pulled back and clasped into a bun at the nape of the neck.

SOURCES OF INFORMATION

Fashion Plates, Victoria and Albert Museum
Costume Gallery, Victoria and Albert Museum

45

1866

1866

1866

1865

1874

1867

1873

1874

1875

1874

1874

1874

1874

46

1865–1875

Variations of these styles continued, tending to become higher on the head, often with a bunch of loose curls, not unlike the modern pony-tail.

By 1867 simplified chignons, sometimes banded with ribbons, were popular with the working classes. However, the upper classes favoured something more complex and by 1874 these styles had reached the height of frivolity. False fronts of curls were worn, mounted perhaps on tulle; twists of hair on wire supports, with crêpe padding, led from each temple and could be plaited high on the back of the head to form a basis for the chignon. This might be based on straw, with a velvet bow at the nape of the neck, and a bunch of curls maybe over thirty inches long adorning the back of the style. This we learn from the French magazine, *Le Moniteur de la Coiffure*.

Long ringlets were fashionable again and the styles decorated with either ribbons, flowers or ostrich feathers. An example is shown of a completely false style, dated 1874. This would fasten at the back of the head, all the ends of hair tucked in behind it to give a natural effect. The other piece of false hair, also dated 1874, is known as a hair plume and worn, for evenings, either alone or in groups of two or three.

SOURCES OF INFORMATION

Le Moniteur de la Coiffure
Fashion Plates, Victoria and Albert Museum

1875

1875

1875

1876

1877

1876

1880

1880

1875

1883

1878

1880

48

1875–1885

Styles continued in the same manner for five years. Two false pieces are illustrated here, both dated 1875. The description of the coiled version reads:

'Twisted chignon in form of a figure eight, placed on the head in such a manner as to represent a diadem in front. A twisted string falling on the nape of the neck whence falls a lock of frizzed and undulated hair sixty to seventy centimetres in length.'†

Le Moniteur de la Coiffure 1875

By 1880 styles had become more severe and probably no false hair would have been used. Either frizzing or small curls to form a fringe seemed popular, the hair then being gently swept back and fastened in a loose chignon at the nape of the neck.

An example for 1883 shows a chignon with a cluster of curls nestled into it. These would in all probability be false.

SOURCES OF INFORMATION

†*Le Moniteur de la Coiffure*
Fashion Plates, Victoria and Albert Museum
Punch History of Manners and Modes

1885

1886

1886

1890

1890

1891

1895

1895

1895

Hair was long and swept up into a variety of chignons. These were secured by decorative pins or a bone version of the modern hairpin.

Fringes were still popular but by 1885 were almost always frizzed into tight waves. Often a few loose curls were worn at the nape of the neck to soften the line. In the evenings, hair would be piled high and decorated with jewels, combs, flowers or birds and butterflies.

By 1890, fringes had developed into two short side curls, falling on either side of the forehead. These were softly curled, in contrast to the severe tight pinning which fastened the hair at the back of the head. Hair on the crown of the head was loosely curled and fell softly onto the forehead. Occasionally a ringlet falling onto the shoulder was favoured by young girls for evening wear.

By 1895 the whole style became softer, with an occasional curl falling onto the forehead, instead of the fringes of previous years. The hair was fluffed out over the temples and caught loosely into a chignon at the back. This gave the effect of a fuller, rounder head of hair, an effect echoed in dress by the 'leg-o'-mutton' sleeves popular at this period.

SOURCES OF INFORMATION

Fashion Prints, Victoria and Albert Museum

1898

1899

1897

1895

1899

1898

1902

1904

1905

1904

1902

'Leg-o'-mutton' sleeves vanished from the fashion scene quite quickly but the 'cloud' effect of hairstyle remained. Variations of this were as follows: firstly, the hair was dressed high into a chignon and puffed out at the sides and back; secondly, the hair was dressed into a roll which ran all round the head, this being built over a wire or horse hair construction. Supports and wire frames were frequently used, and false hair pieces, ready-made into switches, were also popular.

The *'Gibson girl' look* swept America in about 1902, popularized by the fashion artist and cartoonist, Gibson. The accentuated cloud effect was puffed up over wire frames into a roll from temple to temple. This contrasted well with the tiny waists and bustle effects of the period.

By 1905, however, the fullness had diminished and hair was being swept up into a bun at the back, with a slight fullness at the sides, and very often a side or middle parting and a side fringe.

SOURCES OF INFORMATION

Costume Gallery, Victoria and Albert Museum
Mode Feminine de 1900–1920

1905

1909

1910

1910

1912

1913

1913

1909

1915

1913

1915

54

Styles continued for the next few years much the same as those of the last ten years, but by 1910 some of the younger girls were having their hair cut shorter. It was often worn in a loose, fluffed-out style but was sometimes restrained by a bandeau.

By 1912 in France the hair was often very short, and these styles were worn with extravagant high hats during the day and in the evenings decorated with plumes, pearls and bandeaux. In general, however, the older women kept their hair long but wore it low over the ears, to obtain a silhouette similar to that of their shorn daughters.

By 1915 short hair was becoming more and more popular. The hair was cut to sculpture the head at the crown and back. The sides were often slightly longer and trained to form a curl onto the cheek.

SOURCES OF INFORMATION

Mode Feminine de 1900–1920
Gazette du Bon Ton

1917

1916

1922

1919

1922

1920

1919

1919

1920

1922

The First World War was now having a distinct effect on fashion. More and more women were volunteering for war work and looking for more practical fashions in their busy new lives. The short styles, first favoured by the young, became generally popular, and by 1919 scarcely any woman's hair was longer than the ear lobe. The hair was usually swept straight back from the forehead and worn with bandeaux or with a single pearl hanging in the middle of the forehead on a thread or chain. Pearls were extremely popular at this time and often several strings would be suspended from the bandeau to hang under the chin for evening wear. *Toupets* and false pieces were frequently worn to give height to the head in front.

In 1922 a style appeared which may have been favoured by those who had so far refused to cut their hair; this was of cutting the hair at the temples only, so that it fell in soft waves over the ears, the back being made into a chignon.

SOURCES OF INFORMATION

Mode Feminine de 1900–1920
The Queen

1925

1925

1930

1925

1925

1929

1930

1931

1935

In 1925 the short styles had been given names: one was either 'bobbed' (a short style, as in the previous five years) or 'shingled' (this involved the hair being clipped for an inch or so up the back of the neck). When 'bingling' came into fashion—a style in which the hair on the neck was clipped even higher—it was often difficult to make a choice. One can read in *The Queen*, 1925: 'Life was difficult enough when one had to decide between being bobbed or shingled, but now there is another alternative, that of being bingled. It really is easy to understand the state of the Victorian heroes and heroines, who were always being "torn with conflicting emotions" '.

In 1930 hair was still short and still sometimes worn with a longer piece of hair in front of the ear to form a curl on the cheek. By 1931, however, it was fashionable to grow the hair slightly, and have it falling in waves from the forehead and into two or three rolls running round the back of the neck, from one side to the other. False hair pieces and 'transformation pieces' were used. 'Permanent waving' and 'Marcel waving' were increasing in popularity and were to remain popular until the present day. The tightly waved styles were rather a problem to anyone with naturally straight hair and so, in order to follow fashion, these methods of waving were employed.

SOURCES OF INFORMATION

The Queen
Personal records and photographs, and Victoria and Albert Museum

1936

1938

1936

1938

1937

1939

1938

1937

1943

1938

1943

1944

1941 Board of
Trade suggestions

1945

For the first few years, fashions remained unchanged, but with the beginning of the Second World War, British fashions were severely limited. So we can see here a curious mixture of styles: those copied from American magazines of the period are more extravagant, as the Americans did not suffer war shortages. The cinema was also having a tremendous influence on fashion, and the styles worn by film-stars were copied by thousands.

Sausage curls running either from the forehead to the back of the head or in a row along the forehead were popular. The side hair would be caught back tightly at the temples and left to fall either loose or flicked under in a roll from ear to ear, sloping to a point at the back. Sometimes the same front style was used, with the back hair caught up and a mass of sausage curls on top of the head.

The war years persuaded some women to cut their hair for convenience sake, but photographs issued by the Board of Trade to show suitable styles to be worn with uniform hats show long hair either in a plait hanging down and folded under, to be secured at the nape of the neck, or long hair curled into short, sausage-shaped rolls from ear to ear around the nape of the neck.

SOURCES OF INFORMATION

Horst, *Photographs of a Decade*
Louis, *6,000 Years of Hairdressing* (New York Periodical)
Board of Trade photographs
Personal photographs, and Victoria and Albert Museum

1945

1946

1946

1948

1949

1949

1948

1950

1949

1950

1951

1953

1951

1955

The long, loose style was the main one to survive the war years. Popular with film-stars, this was considered to be extremely glamourous and was usually frizzed or curled at the ends. Many women, however, wore their hair simply in a bun at the back of the head, or in a roll right round the top of the head.

In 1945 the 'urchin cut' or 'cap cut' was new and became very popular; the hair was cut very short, like a boy's, and usually left completely straight. However, it was sometimes seen with a slight curl on the cheek. By 1950, younger girls could often be seen with 'pony-tails', the hair being drawn to the back of the head, secured, and allowed to hang free over the shoulders. This style, in a more glamorous form, was popularized by Brigitte Bardot and also noted in one of Picasso's famous paintings.

By 1955 the *bouffant* look was in full swing in America and, within a year or two, became popular in this country. It remained so, in various forms, for six or seven years and involved the hair being 'back-brushed' or 'back-combed' until it was standing on end all over the head and then brushed down gently, to form a 'puff-ball' around the face.

SOURCES OF INFORMATION

Vogue Pattern Book
Vogue
Hair Style

1955

1957

1960

1957

1960

1959

1960

1960

64

So much information is available for this period that I have used two pages in order to show a good selection of styles. They have been chosen to try to show both the extremes for evening and day wear and the styles most commonly worn.

1955–1960

From 1955 onwards the *bouffant* style was fashionable and indeed is still worn today in various forms. As has been mentioned before, this was achieved by 'back-combing', lifting up sections of hair and pulling the comb rapidly through from tip to root to give the hair more body. If badly done, this can cause tangles, but if done professionally, it is not harmful to the hair. When the hair had been treated in this way, very high or full styles could be obtained without the use of false hair.

Another completely contrasting style was that of absolutely straight hair, cut in a fringe on the forehead and hanging down to shoulder length or slightly below. An alternative to this style was to have the ends curled upwards into 'flick-ups'.

Straight hair was now in vogue, a complete contrast to the styles of thirty years before, when permanent waving became popular. Girls and women with straight hair found themselves better able to follow high fashion styles and de-frizzing (the opposite of permanent waving) became possible for those with curly hair.

SOURCES OF INFORMATION

Quentin Crewe, *The Frontiers of Privilege*
Vogue
Vogue Pattern Book
Personal Records, and Victoria and Albert Museum

1964

1960

1961

1960

1962

1963

1961

66

1960–1965

During this period false hair pieces became available for those who could afford them, and grew in popularity during the five years. Where in previous years all false hair pieces had been hand-made, now it was possible to make parts of them by machine, which meant that the prices became lower and more people could buy them. However, the best pieces would still be hand-made.

Smooth, sleek styles remained popular, and by 1963 upswept styles were favoured by many, with often quite complicated styles for evening, usually involving false hair pieces.

During 1963 another style which became popular, particularly with young people, was that of a straight cut with a graded back, cut in layers. This demanded a high standard of cutting and also constant attention to keep it in shape.

The 'Cleopatra Look' in 1963 was copied by thousands, and again fringes were worn with long, straight hair to the shoulders. This was a short-lived craze, however, influenced originally by a film and dying out quite naturally after a few months.

By 1964 the trend was more towards short hair for teenagers who followed fashion. This trend probably began as a compliment to the boys' styles, which were shoulder length. These styles, however, were only copied by a few, and, as in the case of any other extreme style, it will be interesting to see how long they last.

SOURCES OF INFORMATION

Vogue
Vogue Pattern Book
Hair & Beauty

Accessories & Jewellery

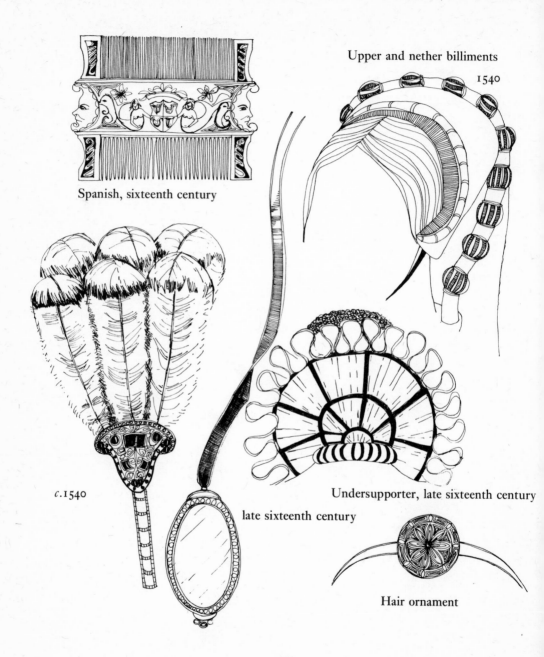

Spanish, sixteenth century

Upper and nether billiments
1540

c.1540

late sixteenth century

Undersupporter, late sixteenth century

Hair ornament

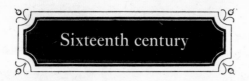
The comb, in use since earliest times, had by this period developed into a two-sided ornamental piece, sometimes made of wood but usually of bone or ivory. The teeth were of a different width at each side and, although hand-carved, extremely regular. Some considered that lead combs improved the colour of the hair.

The hair was usually covered, head-dresses often being a development of both head-dress and circlets previously worn by a bride or young girl. Circlets in bandeau form were called *billiments*, upper and nether, and were of gold and silver, often decorated with jewels, or in the form of separate gold beads threaded on a rouleau of velvet or satin. The billiments were interchangeable and could be attached to the cap or hood, presumably by pins.

Often *fans* would be carried, to ward off germs and evil smells as much as to keep the owner cool. It was also modish to carry, hanging from the waist on long ribbons, mirrors (as illustrated), small phials containing powders, or '*Spanish papers*' (small pieces of paper covered with powder for the face), and sometimes *pomanders* (aromatic balls made from Seville oranges, stuck with cloves).

By the latter half of the century, the fashion for built-up hairstyles and high ruffs or lace collars made necessary some kind of support. The miniatures and portraits of the period usually present the front view. At the back, hardly ever seen, the ruff or collar was starched and supported on a metal framework placed around the neck like a yoke. The arrangement must have been exceedingly uncomfortable and necessitated a good upright posture.

Pearl hair ornament
1600–1615

Sixteenth or
seventeenth century

Top knot 1689–1690

Pair of hair ornaments
seventeenth century

Half mask early seventeenth century

Embroidered cap
seventeenth century

Patches 1672–1675

As the fashion for high styles continued, so hair ornaments grew in popularity. They were often made of pearls set in gold or silver, as illustrated, attached to pins or bodkins and stuck into the hair. Several small pieces might be worn at once, giving a spangled effect.

Masks were widely worn, the one shown being of black velvet and tying around the head by tapes. Masks protected make-up from the weather, for the application of make-up was costly. Its corrosive effects have been mentioned: in order to disguise boils and pimples, *patches* were worn, stuck over blemishes with mastic, made of black silk and cut to a variety of shapes.

By 1625 hairstyles had diminished in size, and ruffs and collars disappeared. Ringlets became fashionable and hair ornaments were designed accordingly. The pair opposite was made of rows of pearls suspended in loops from a large jewelled button, worn on either side of the head above the bunches of ringlets covering the ears. The embroidered cap, of traditional design, is in deep reds and greens on a pale cream background. This would be worn with a simpler hairstyle than most of those described, probably by a middle-class woman.

It must be remembered that the fashions in paintings are those of wealthy women, which most of the middle and lower classes could not afford to follow.

By the end of the century, the *fontange* was popular, named after the Duchesse de Fontange, a favourite of King Louis XIV mentioned in the Foreword. Worn with the style were a variety of starched pleated ruffs and ribbon loops, and in England a slightly modified version of these loops, called a top knot.

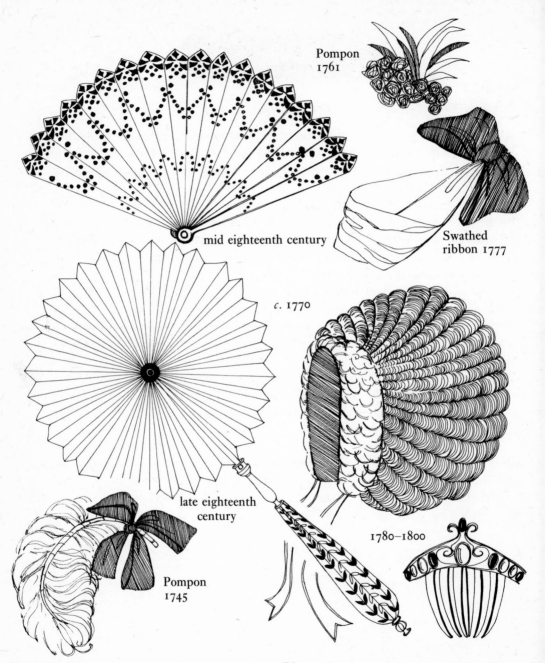

Pompon
1761

Swathed
ribbon 1777

mid eighteenth century

c. 1770

late eighteenth
century

Pompon
1745

1780–1800

74

Early in the century, hairstyles were close to the head and decorated with ribbon bows and artificial flowers, these often as made-up pieces called pompons, with feathers, pearls or lace.

The fan was popular throughout the century, made in practically every fabric, from paper and vellum to satin and silk, usually decorative and often painted. Laces and brocades were popular, as were feathers, horn and ivory. Most fans were of a set shape (a third of a circle), differing in size, but some were circular (as in the illustration), attached to a long decorative handle inlaid with gold and silver.

By about 1750 ladies were using perukes or wigs, unlike those worn by men, some shaped like small caps over which pads and false hair were arranged, others being complete wigs which could be sent to the hairdressers—otherwise ladies often had to have their hair arranged the night before an event and found sleeping extremely difficult. Powder was blown onto the hair through a tube while the lady covered her face.

As styles reached fantastic heights, different decorations were used by each individual. Tulle, feathers and ribbons were all popular at different stages of the period.

In 1769 there were over a thousand hairdressers in Paris, often taking pupils and charging fees for tuition. They would visit ladies at home, male hairdressers being greatly preferred to female.

The comb illustrated was worn as an evening decoration towards 1800, although for daytime hair had become much shorter and bonnets were often worn.

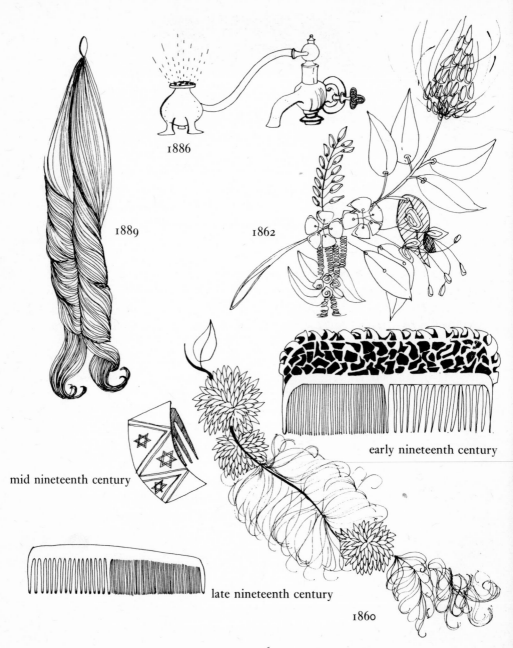

1886

1889

1862

early nineteenth century

mid nineteenth century

late nineteenth century

1860

76

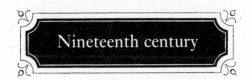

The nineteenth century was a period of great change in hair accessories. *Combs* had become one-sided, with the teeth of different width at either end, and by the end of the century they were mass produced in a similar form to those of today. Also shown is a Chinese ivory comb with an intricate carved design.

False hair pieces were worn at certain stages of the century: the one shown here is of curled ringlets in a switch form, made in the same way as a modern switch, either of curly hair or of straight hair which could be curled. It would be attached by a wire loop and hairpin.

In mid-century hair ornaments were popular. The one illustrated was made in the West Indies, dated 1862, entirely of shells, assembled into a floral design by fine wire. Some of the shells are attached to springs, thus dancing with every movement of the head. Similar ornaments would be frequent evening wear, like the one illustrated opposite made of ostrich feathers and artificial flowers, formed into a spray and attached by a hairpin. The comb decoration shown, made of tortoise-shell inlaid with silver, could be worn with almost any style.

Make-up was not widely used around 1800, English women being much more reticent in this respect than the French. Eventually older ladies began using home-made recipes and the fashion was again set. By 1870 however make-up was considered improper, the only beauty aid being to cleanse the skin by steaming the face.

In the 1860s *curling tongs* were used even on children's hair to follow the fashion of curls and ringlets.

Hairpins early in the century were usually brass and still a luxury.

During the latter half of the century *hairdressing salons* appeared, usually built on a cubicle basis, although sometimes the basins would be together in one block, as today. The idea of the salon was a great step towards the present attitude to hairdressing. Hitherto it would have been unheard of for a young girl to visit such an establishment, and, unless she could afford personal visits from a hairdresser, she would have done her hair herself or hired a maid.

The *shampoo spray*, advertised in 1875, would be fastened to the tap by a rubber tube, the spray standing at the bottom of the basin, spraying upwards.

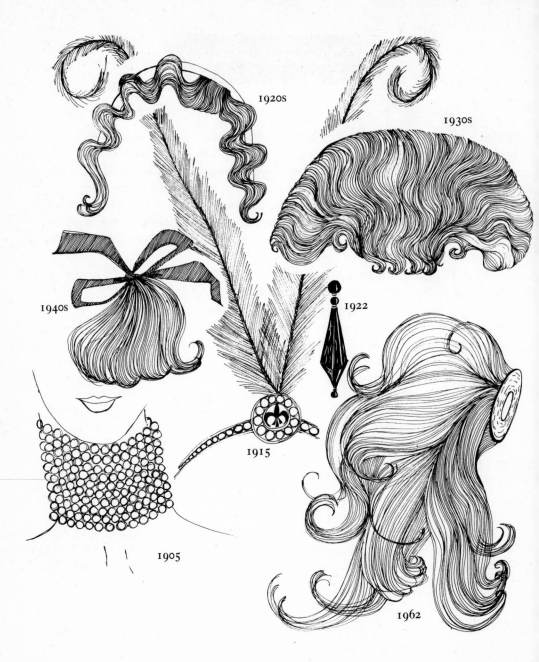

1920S

1930S

1940S

1922

1915

1905

1962

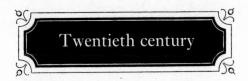

Hairdressing salons so became an everyday sight that by the 1960s each town had several, with a regular clientele.

The popularity of bleached hair diminished, and auburn tints became accepted. Steel hairpins were used, until the introduction of the 'invisible' hairpin, and decorative pins of tortoise-shell, horn and celluloid.

Before 1950 *pearls* were considered smart, worn as single ball ear-rings or as high choker necklaces. *Lorgnettes*, in tortoise-shell or gold and silver, with round lenses, were likewise fashionable.

By 1915 there had been a change towards waved styles and false hair pieces. The two illustrated both show additions to the front of the head: the *'light frontlet'* being smaller and fastened to a bandeau round the head; the *'Pompadour postiche'* a fuller piece, attached to the usual net backing, to add height or disguise receding and greying hair at the temples; both would be mingled with existing hair.

With the advent of shorter styles, *bandeaux* were worn low across the forehead, often made of gold or silver, sometimes of ribbons, and usually decorated with tall plumes of feathers.

Jet, popular in the 1800s, returned to fashion in the 1920s to replace pearls among the younger set, often imitation as 'costume jewellery' became accepted.

During the 1940s false hair pieces were worn when available, usually small and sometimes attached to ribbon bows.

Make-up was accepted by the twenties, and made from pure ingredients, beneficial to the complexion. The mouth was painted larger than normal during the 'thirties for the first time.

Brooches and ear-rings with either clip or screw fastenings were worn, sometimes a pair of brooches to decorate the neckline of a dress.

Between 1950 and 1965 wigs, considered to be a revolutionary idea, returned increasingly to fashion for special effects.

List of Books, Periodicals and Museums
used for reference

BOOKS

G. Aretz	*The Elegant Woman* (George Harrap)
C. W. and P. Cunnington	*Handbook of English Mediaeval Costume*
J. Evans	*Dress in Mediaeval France* (Oxford, at the Clarendon Press)
E. Gardner	*Hair and Headdress* (British Architects Journal)
H. H. Hansen	*Costume Cavalcade*
Hilaire and Meyer	*Bibliography of Costume*
Horst	*Photographs of a Decade*
M. Houston	*Mediaeval Costume in England and France* (Adam and Charles Black)
Kelly	*Shakespearean Costume for Stage and Screen* (Adam and Charles Black)
F. Kelly and R. Schwabe	*Historic Costume* (Batsford)
J. Laver	*Costume Through the Ages*
Louis	*The History of Hairstyles*
Louis	*6,000 Years of Hairstyling* (New York Periodical)
Lunguist	*La Mode et son Vocabulaire*
Norris	*Costume and Fashion* (J. M. Dent)
Racinet	*Le Costume* (*Librairie de Fiemin Didot et Cie*)
Sronkova	*Gothic Women's Fashion* (Artia, Prague)
Stephané	*L'Art de la Coiffure Féminine* (Édition de 'La Coiffure de Paris')
Stewart	*The Whole Art of Hairdressing*
Stewart	*Ploscasmos*
Strömbom,	*Index över Svenska Porträtt 1500–1850* (Catalogues of Stockholm National Museum)
R. Turner-Wilcox	*The Mode of Hats and Headdresses* (Charles Scribner's Sons, New York)

PERIODICALS

Cahier de Modes 1950–1951
Coiffure European
Costume Gothic and Renaissance (New York Public Library)
Gazette du Bon Ton
La Mode Féminine de 1900 à 1920
Les Modes
Le Moniteur de la Coiffure
The Queen
Vogue
Vogue Pattern Book
Hair and Beauty
Hair Fashion

MUSEUMS AND LIBRARIES USED FOR REFERENCE

Victoria and Albert Museum Print Room, Miniature Room, Costume Gallery, Library, Wood Carvings.

Bethnal Green Museum
National Gallery
National Portrait Gallery
Hertfordshire County Libraries

Suggestions for Further Sources of Information

This list indicates the situation of museums and galleries in Great Britain and Ireland that contain material which may be of interest to readers of this book. (For author's references to actual material used, see pages 81–2.)

Abergavenny, Monmouthshire	Prints, costumes
Abingdon, Berkshire	Sixteenth to eighteenth century costumes
Accrington, Lancashire	Water colours
Arbroath, Angus	Pastels and water colours
Bangor, Caernarvon	Costumes and prints
Bath, Somerset	Museum of Costume (every aspect of costume since seventeenth century)
Blithfield, Staffordshire	Costumes
Burnley, Lancashire	Costumes, accessories, prints and water colours
Chelmsford, Essex	Costumes, paintings
Christchurch, Hampshire	Nineteenth century fashion plates
Colchester, Essex	Costume, eighteenth century settings
Dunfermline, Fife	Nineteenth century costumes, prints
Edinburgh, Midlothian	Highland dress, eighteenth and nineteenth century costume
Gateshead, County Durham	Oil and water colours
Glasgow, Lanarkshire	Costume, oil and water colours
Guernsey, Channel Islands	Costume
Halifax, Yorkshire	Costume and textiles
Hereford, Herefordshire	Costume and paintings
Hove, Sussex	Fine art of 1700–1851 and costume
Kilmarnock, Ayrshire	Oil and water colours
Kings Lynn, Norfolk	Costume, oil and water colours
Kingussie, Inverness	Highland dress
Leeds, Yorkshire	Museum depicting the lives of people of Yorkshire since 1665
Leicester, Leicestershire	Costume
Lewes, Sussex	Prints and water colours
Liverpool, Lancashire	Eighteenth and nineteenth century paintings, costume

83

London, Bethnal Green Museum	Costume
Geffrye Museum	Photographs of costumes
London Museum	Royal robes and costume
National Gallery	Paintings
National Portrait Gallery	Paintings and drawings
Victoria and Albert Museum	Costumes, prints and library miniatures
Luton, Bedfordshire	Details of hat industry
Manchester, Lancashire	Gallery of English costume
Newcastle-under-Lyme, Staffordshire	Water colours
Newcastle-upon-Tyne, Northumberland	Paintings and water colours, costumes
Northampton, Northamptonshire	Water colours
Oldham, Lancashire	Nineteenth and twentieth century water colour paintings
Oxford, Ashmolean Museum	Prints, paintings, water colours, engraved portraits
Preston, Lancashire	Costume, colour prints, paintings
Salisbury, Wiltshire	Costume
Totnes, Devon	Costume
Wakefield, Yorkshire	Eighteenth century water colours, costume
Warwick, Warwickshire	Costume
Worthing, Sussex	Costume, early English water colours
Yeovil, Somerset	Bailward costume collection
York, Yorkshire	Costumes

Index

Attifet Coiffure, 6, 7

Back-combing, 7, 10, 11, 63, 65
Bandeau, 32–35, 37, 55, 56, 79
Billiments, 70, 71
Bingle, 58, 59
Bleaching, 79
Bob, 56, 58, 59
Bonnet, 26, 27, 35, 48, 72, 75
Bouffant, 62–65
Braids, 40, 41, 46
Brooches, 79
Bun, 12–20, 23, 27, 30, 31, 37, 40, 46, 53

Cap, 73
Chignon, 29, 33–37, 39, 42, 46
Chignon Flotant, 28–31
Cleopatra look, 66–67
'Cloud' hairstyle, 52, 53
Coif, 3, 13
Coiffure, 29
Comb, 43, 46, 48, 70, 72, 75–77
Confidants, 18, 19
Cosmetics, 7
Crève-Coeurs, 18, 19
Cruches, 18, 19
Curling tongs, 77
Curls, 14–16, 31, 35, 41, 44–49, 51
Cushions, 28, 29, 41, 43, 47, 49, 51, 57
Cutting, 66, 67

De-frizzing, 65
'Dishevelled' look, 32–35

Ear-rings, 78, 79

Face painting, 7, 9
Face patches, 15, 72, 73
False hair pieces, 39, 46, 49, 59, 67, 76–79, 64, 65
Fans, 70, 71, 74, 75
Favourites, 18–21
Feathers, 11
Flick-ups, 64–65
Fontange, 20, 21, 23, 73
Fringe, 12–17, 30–35, 50, 51
Frizzing, 6, 7, 10, 14, 15, 48–51

'Gibson Girl' look, 52, 53

Hair decorations, 15, 16, 37, 39, 46, 48, 70, 72, 73, 76, 77
Hairdressers, 75
Hairdressing salons, 77, 79
Hairpin, 43, 54, 77, 79
Hair plume, 46, 47
Hanover cut, 22, 23
Hats, 35–39, 52–55
Head-dresses, 2–9, 27

Jet, 78, 79
Jewels, 11

Light frontlet, 78, 79
Lorgnettes, 79
Loup mask, 7

Make-up, 77, 79
Marcel waving, 58, 59
Masks, 7, 9, 72, 73
Mirrors, 70, 71
Mob caps, 24–27, 30, 31
Mucelage, 7

Ostrich plumes, 36, 37, 46, 47, 50, 53, 76

Pads, 9, 15, 29
Passagère, 18, 19
Paste, 7, 29, 31
Pearls, 11, 16–19, 26, 27, 41, 79
Periwig, 7, 10, 11, 13, 24, 25, 27, 75, 79
Permanent waving, 58, 59, 65
Peruke, 7, 74, 75
Plait, 27, 35–37, 48
Poke bonnet, 42–44
Pomanders, 71
Pomatum, 23, 29
Pompadour postiche, 78, 79
Pompons, 74, 75
Pony-tail, 62, 63
Powdering, 7, 21, 23, 75
Puffs, 15, 31, 38, 39, 45, 59, 63

Ribbons, 74–75
Ringlets, 12–17, 19, 21, 23, 30, 31, 37–46, 48–51
Rolls, 14, 15, 21, 23, 29
Roses, 36, 37, 42, 46
Ruff, 8, 9, 70

Sausage curls, 37, 44–46, 60, 61
Shampoo spray, 76, 77
Shingle, 56, 57, 59
Spanish papers, 71
Switches, 52, 53

Tête-de-mouton, 24–27
Toupee, 28, 29
Toupet, 56–58
Tour, 20, 21
Transformation pieces, 59, 88
Tulle, 47, 75

Urchin cut, 62, 63

Veil, 12, 13, 39

Wig, 7, 31
Wired-out curls, 18, 19, 21
Wire supports, 12, 13, 47, 53, 70, 71